Dear Dr. Bell...
Your friend,
Helen Keller

Dear Dr. Bell...
Your friend,
Helen Keller

· ·

JUDITH ST. GEORGE

illustrated with photographs

Copy 1

G. P. PUTNAM'S SONS   NEW YORK

G. P. Putnam's Sons, a division of The Putnam & Grosset Group,
200 Madison Avenue, New York, NY 10016.
Published simultaneously in Canada.
Printed in the United States of America.
Book design by Kathleen Westray.

Library of Congress Cataloging-in-Publication Data
St. George, Judith, date
Dear Dr. Bell . . . your friend, Helen Keller/Judith St. George.
p.   cm.
Includes bibliographical references and index.
Summary: Follows the parallel lives of Helen Keller and
Alexander Graham Bell, who continued to encounter and support
each other from that eventful meeting when he recommended
she be given a teacher and thus led her to Annie Sullivan.
1. Keller, Helen, 1880-1968—Friends and associates—Juvenile literature.
2. Blind-Deaf—United States—Biography—Juvenile literature.
3. Bell, Alexander Graham, 1847-1922—Friends and associates—
Juvenile literature. [1. Keller, Helen, 1880-1968. 2. Blind.
3. Deaf. 4. Physically handicapped. 5. Bell, Alexander Graham, 1847-1922.
6. Inventors.] I. Title. II. Title: Dear Doctor Bell.
HV1624.K4S7   1992   362.4'1'092—dc20
[B]   91-37327   CIP   AC

ISBN 0-399-22337-1

10   9   8   7   6   5   4   3   2

TO EMILY ANNE, WITH LOVE

· · · · ·

Acknowledgments:

With grateful thanks to Alberta Lonergan, Archivist of the Helen Keller Archives, American Foundation for the Blind; Judith Anderson, Librarian of the Volta Bureau Library, Alexander Graham Bell Association for the Deaf; Maja Keech, Reference Specialist, Prints and Photographs Division, the Library of Congress, and the staff of the Manuscript Division, the Library of Congress, for all their help in the telling of this story.

CHAPTER *1*

. . . . .

T HE LITTLE six-year-old girl could hardly contain her excitement at being on her first long train trip during that summer of 1886. She was traveling with her father and her Aunt Ev all the way from Alabama to Baltimore, Maryland. The time passed quickly as the train clickety-clacked through small southern towns, stopping often to take on passengers, fuel and water.

The child made friends with almost everyone on the train. One passenger gave her a box of shells, which she patiently strung into a long necklace. The conductor, who took a special liking to the child, allowed her to hang on to his coattails as he made his rounds collecting tickets. And when he wasn't using his ticket punch, the little girl curled up in a corner and used the punch to make holes in scraps of cardboard.

The doll that Aunt Ev fashioned out of old towels wasn't so successful. It was a silly, shapeless thing without eyes, ears, nose or mouth. The child was especially upset that the doll had no eyes, but no one seemed to know how to solve the problem until the child herself pulled her aunt's cape out from under the seat, ripped off two large beads, and indicated that she wanted the beads sewn on the doll for eyes.

It was no wonder that the doll's lack of eyes distressed six-year-old Helen Keller. Helen herself was blind. More than that, she couldn't hear the shriek of the train whistle or the wheels tapping over the tracks. She couldn't chat with the other passengers, or pester her father about how much farther they had to go. When she was an infant, Helen Keller had been struck by an illness that had left her blind, deaf and unable to speak. At least she had learned to communicate by making signs: A hand on her cheek meant Mother and putting on eyeglasses meant Father. Now, her father, Captain Arthur Keller, and her Aunt Eveline Keller were taking Helen to Baltimore to consult with a famous eye doctor, who just might be able to restore her sight.

But the famous doctor held out no hope for Helen's eyes. Instead, sensing that Helen was a bright child, he advised Captain Keller to get in touch with Alexander Graham Bell, who had not only invented the telephone ten years earlier, but was also deeply committed to the education of the deaf, especially deaf children. Desperate to do anything that might help Helen, Captain Keller made an appointment to see Bell in his Washington, D.C., home.

Bell, who looked forward to the meeting, sent a note to a fellow teacher of the deaf. "Mr. A. H. Keller of Alabama will dine with me this evening and bring with him his little daughter (age about 6½) who is deaf and blind and has been so from nearly infancy. He is in search of light regarding methods of education. The little girl is evidently an intelligent child."

Years later, Helen recalled that first meeting with Bell. "He held me on his knee while I examined his watch, and he made it strike for me. He understood my signs, and I knew it and loved him at once," she wrote. "From that moment until his death my life was greatly blessed by his understanding and love."

A unique connection had been made between the world-famous inventor and the silent little girl from Alabama that would grow into a lifelong friendship. And just as Alexander Graham Bell's telephone had broken down the barriers of isolation between people around the world, so, too, did Helen Keller's first meeting with Bell launch her on her own journey of breaking down the barriers that isolated the deaf, the blind and the handicapped everywhere.

The family dog is a comfort to seven-year-old Helen
in her dark and silent world.

• • • • •

CHAPTER *2*

. . . . .

"**M**R. WATSON —Come here—I want to see you."

The world hasn't been the same since Alexander Graham Bell spoke those words to his assistant over the first working telephone on March 10, 1876. With Bell's invention of the telephone, human communication was changed forever.

Alexander Bell, who was born on March 3, 1847, in Edinburgh, Scotland, was interested in speech and communication from early childhood, as well he might have been. Young Aleck's grandfather, whom he was named after, was an actor and a well-known teacher of the art of speaking, known in those days as elocution. His father, Alexander Melville Bell, was not only an elocutionist and professor of speech, but he had also worked twenty years to create a new system of teaching the correct way to speak, which he called Visible Speech.

The fact that Aleck's mother, Eliza Bell, was almost totally deaf and could hear only with the aid of a rubber ear tube further sparked Aleck's interest in speech and sound. Gifted with a rich and melodious voice, the boy was able to communicate with his mother better than anyone in the family by speaking in low tones close to her forehead. Both Aleck and his mother were fine pianists, and Bell later observed that "my early passion for music had a good deal to do in preparing me for the scientific study of sound." And it was his mother who first taught Aleck the double-hand manual alphabet, a method of communication that used both hands to spell out the letters of the alphabet.

When Aleck was ten, he decided that he wanted a middle name to distinguish himself from his father and grandfather. At the time, a young man named Alexander Graham was boarding with the Bells and the combination of the two names so appealed to Aleck that on his eleventh birthday, he took the middle name of Graham.

As a student, Aleck's record was never better than average. His mother taught him (and his two brothers) at home until he entered a local academy at the age of ten. The following year he went on to Edinburgh's Royal High School, finishing his course of studies in four years. Although Aleck had friends among the other boys, he treasured time alone and often climbed the hills outside Edinburgh to dream and watch the gulls soar overhead. "In boyhood," he wrote, "I have spent many happy hours lying among the heather on the Scottish hills—breathing in the scenery around me with a quiet delight that is even now pleasant for me to remember."

After he finished his schooling, Aleck spent his fifteenth year in London with his grandfather, Alexander Bell, who awakened in the boy a lifelong interest in books and learning, as well as instilling in him strong moral and ethical values. That year, Bell declared almost fifty years later, was "the turning point of my whole career."

Upon his return to Scotland in 1863, Aleck, at the age of sixteen, followed in the footsteps of his grandfather, father, uncle and older brother to become a teacher of speech (and music), first in Scotland and then in England. But being only a teacher wasn't enough for Aleck. As a boy, he had invented a machine to take the husks off wheat, while in his teens, he and his brother had designed a crude "speaking machine." Now, when his workday was over, he experimented at night with different shapings of his mouth and throat to produce sounds that would make tuning forks vibrate. He tinkered, too, with

At the age of sixteen, Aleck Bell begins his teaching career in Elgin, Scotland, 1863.

• • • • •

electrical batteries and telegraphic instruments, all of which, unknown to him at the time, was laying the groundwork for his future invention of the telephone.

When Aleck was twenty-one, a whole new future opened up to him. In 1868, A. Graham Bell, as he called himself, began teaching speech and lipreading to four deaf children in London. Aleck's pupils, whom he described as "remarkably intelligent happy-looking little girls," responded immediately to his instruction and could soon speak well enough to be understood. It was Aleck's success with them, and his delight at their success, that launched him on "what proved to be my life-work— the teaching of speech to the deaf." His devotion to the deaf never wavered. No matter what fame and honors were ever bestowed on Bell, he always proudly listed his profession as "teacher of the deaf."

During that period, the Bell family was struck by a double tragedy. In 1867, Aleck's younger brother died of tuberculosis. Three years later, his older brother died of the same disease. After their second son's death, Aleck's parents, who had moved to London in 1865, made the decision to emigrate to Canada. Worried about Aleck, who had never been strong, and who suffered from bad headaches, especially in hot weather, Eliza and Melville Bell urged their only surviving son to come with them to Canada in the hopes that a more vigorous climate might improve his health. Although Aleck had begun studies at the University of London, and was happily teaching speech to deaf children, he reluctantly agreed. In the summer of 1870, at the age of twenty-three, Aleck sailed with his parents to Canada.

At their new home near Brantford, Ontario, Aleck's health improved so much that the following year he took a job teaching Visible Speech in Boston at a new public school run by Sarah Fuller, called the Boston School for Deaf Mutes. Instead of letters, the Visible Speech alphabet, devised by Aleck's father, was made up of thirty-four symbols, with each symbol showing how the throat, tongue, mouth and teeth should be positioned in order to make certain sounds.

Aleck's thirty-some deaf pupils won him over instantly . . .

[ENGLISH ALPHABET OF VISIBLE SPEECH,

Expressed in the Names of Numbers and Objects.]

[Pronounce the Nos.]	[Names.]	[Name the Objects.]		[Name the Objects.]	
1.					
2.					
3.					
4.					
5.					
6.					
7.					
8.					

[EXERCISE.]

One by one.
Two or three.
Four at once.
Five o'clock.
Half-past six.
Seven-thirty.
Eight to nine.
Ten or twelve.
Twice two, four.
Twice three, six.
Four and four, eight.
Nine and two, eleven.
Twice or thrice.

Two, a couple.
Twelve, a dozen.
Twenty, a score.
A book-case.
A few books.
New book-shelves.
A silver watch.
A gold watch.
The watch-key.
A good saw.
Cap and feather.
Tongs and shovel.
Sugar-tongs.

A hunting whip.
A table lamp.
A bunch of onions.
Corns and bunions.
A ship's boat.
A sailing boat.
Cart and horse.
A round tent.
Rows of houses.
A dog-kennel.
A little monkey.
A pretty cage.
A green canary.

Alexander Graham Bell's father devised the Visible Speech
alphabet in 1864 after fifteen years of effort.

· · · · ·

and he won them over. With his jet black hair and deep, dark eyes, combined with a beautiful speaking voice, the tall, handsome Aleck Bell not only charmed his young students, but the rest of Boston, too. And his career flourished. Although Aleck had never finished his university courses, in 1873 he was appointed professor of "Vocal Physiology and Elocution" at Boston University, a position which earned him prestige in Boston's scientific circles. Meanwhile, his growing reputation for teaching Visible Speech to the deaf brought him private students, as well as teaching jobs at the Clarke School for the Deaf in Northampton, Massachusetts, and the American Asylum for Deaf Mutes in Hartford, Connecticut.

"My feelings and sympathies are every day more and more aroused," he wrote home to his father about his deaf pupils. "It makes my very heart ache to see the difficulties the little children have to contend with." Anxious to do anything that might help his students, Aleck learned sign language, although he never approved of it as a method of communication for the deaf.

As if his busy schedule weren't enough, Aleck began experimenting at night after work on an invention called a multiple telegraph system, which would allow a number of telegraph messages to be sent over a single wire at the same time. Aleck's routine of working until 3 or 4 A.M., which he had begun as a schoolteacher in Scotland, became a lifetime practice of staying up most of the night and sleeping until late morning. Demanding total quiet during those night hours, he even turned off clock chimes. No matter how hard he tried, or how much his family nagged him, he could never break himself of the habit. "To take night from me is to rob me of *life*," he once admitted. How similar that night silence was to the silent world of the deaf and the night darkness was to the dark world of the blind. Certainly the isolation of the night echoed the isolation experienced by both groups.

Just as the boy Aleck once lay on the hills of Edinburgh and dreamed as he watched the gulls glide and wheel overhead, so the young man Aleck lay on a bluff near his parents' Brantford home on lazy summer days and watched the Grand River mean-

Students and teachers gather on the front steps of the Boston School for Deaf Mutes in 1871 (Bell, top right).

• • • • •

der below. This quiet spot was what he called his "dreaming place." Bell once remarked: "Discoveries and inventions arise from the observation of little things." And for him it was true.

In the summer of 1874, a simple but brilliant idea struck Aleck while at his "dreaming place." He already knew many of the principles of sound: singing into a piano would cause the strings to echo back; sound waves could move small bones in the ear; a sound vibrating a metal plate could make or break an electrical circuit. It wasn't as if these principles weren't already known. They were. But only Alexander Graham Bell thought to combine them into a single working unit by asking why vibrations from the human voice couldn't be transmitted and received electrically by thin metal disks called diaphragms. The telephone was born, at least in Aleck's mind.

Although two businessmen, Gardiner Greene Hubbard and Thomas Sanders, were financing Aleck to work on perfecting the multiple telegraph, when Aleck returned to Boston in the fall of 1874, he began spending all of his nighttime hours developing the telephone. An added complication in Aleck's life was that he had fallen in love with Gardiner Greene Hubbard's deaf daughter, Mabel, who had been his pupil for two years. "I have learned to love her," the twenty-seven-year-old Aleck wrote to Mabel's mother.

Although an attack of scarlet fever at the age of five had left Mabel completely deaf, she had learned to lip-read, which was almost unheard of at the time, and was improving her speech under Aleck's instruction. But the Hubbards objected to the match. They thought that at seventeen, Mabel was too young and that Aleck's future was much too uncertain. Hubbard scolded Aleck for his eagerness "to undertake every new thing that interests you & accomplish nothing of any value to any one." Hubbard even offered Mabel's hand in marriage, plus living expenses, if Aleck would drop his work with Visible Speech and the deaf and concentrate on inventing. Absolutely not! Much as Aleck loved Mabel, nothing could make him give up his commitment to the deaf. "Of one thing I become more sure every day—that my interest in the Deaf is to be a life-long thing with me," Aleck wrote to Mabel. "I shall never leave this work."

At last, with the Hubbards' grudging approval, Aleck and Mabel became engaged on Thanksgiving Day, 1875. (To tease Aleck about his late-night habits, Mabel's promise to paint his portrait turned out to be a painting of a great white owl.) By this time, both Hubbard and Sanders, whose deaf son was also Aleck's pupil, had become interested in his experiments with the telephone. Although Aleck had hired an expert electrician, twenty-year-old Thomas Watson, to assist him, he was still too busy to do anything about applying for a telephone patent. "I rush from one thing to another and before I know it the day has gone!" Aleck grumbled to his parents.

Finally Hubbard himself filed for the patent, which was issued on March 7, 1876, just four days after Aleck's twenty-ninth birthday and three days before he spoke his famous first words to Watson.

Patent No. 174,465 is generally considered to be the most valuable patent ever issued. The Greek roots of the word telephone mean "far-speaking," which says it all. The telephone, which became an extension of the human body, a listening ear and a speaking voice, became the most important means of communication in the world, affecting every aspect of life. Quickly replacing the mails and the telegraph, the telephone enabled families and friends separated by a continent to chat as if they were on their front porches. Police, fire and emergency services could be summoned immediately. Businesses were able to set up conference calls around the country to exchange ideas, while in times of crisis world leaders could communicate with each other instantly. Ironically, three of the women dearest to Bell, his mother, his wife and Helen Keller, were never able to use his invention without assistance.

In July 1877, Bell, Watson, Hubbard and Sanders formed the Bell Telephone Company, which eventually expanded into the multibillion-dollar American Telephone and Telegraph Company, the world's largest single business enterprise. Perhaps even more important, the words that Bell spoke to Watson opened the way to a communication network that linked people and nations into such a giant family, that the huge A.T. and T. Company acquired the all-embracing nickname of Ma Bell. (In 1984, A.T. and T. was broken up into seven smaller companies known as the Baby Bells.)

The ten years following Bell's invention of the telephone were full ones. A "glorious success" was how Bell described the demonstration of his telephone at the 1876 centennial celebration of America's independence in Philadelphia. A year later, on July 7, 1877, Aleck and Mabel were married, spending the next year and a half in Scotland and England, where Bell lectured,

Handsome Aleck Bell is slender and dark-haired the year
he invents the telephone, 1876.

• • • • •

MT. VERNON MIDDLE SCHOOL

visited schools for the deaf and demonstrated his telephone. A London newspaper described Bell's private demonstration for Queen Victoria: "Being a handsome man and a fluent speaker Professor Bell completely held the attention of the Queen, who evinced the greatest pleasure the moment the telephone was put to the test."

Mabel, who had earlier convinced her husband to drop the "k" from Aleck, now urged him to use his full name instead of the "A. Graham Bell" of his younger days. It would, after all, match his impressive new appearance, which had expanded by an additional thirty-five or forty pounds and a full black beard. Despite his growing girth and fame, Bell continued to remain a very private person, declaring truthfully that his lovely wife Mabel was "the chief link between myself and the world." The Bells had two daughters, Elsie and Marian (known as Daisy), as well as two sons, both of whom were born prematurely and died shortly after birth, a loss that Alec and Mabel mourned for the rest of their lives.

After returning to America in late 1878, the Bells moved to Washington, D.C. Comfortably well-off, but not in the million-aire class as everyone assumed, Bell immediately embarked on new experiments with the statement that an inventor "can no more help inventing than he can help thinking or breathing." In recognition of his work with the telephone, the French government awarded Bell the renowned Volta Prize in 1880 for his scientific achievement in electricity. Bell used all the $10,000 prize money to establish what he called the Volta Laboratory in Washington, D.C., where he continued to carry out his experiments.

Bell's inventions ranged from an audiometer, which tested hearing ability, to the photophone, which transmitted sound a short distance by a beam of light, to a commercial improvement on Thomas Edison's phonograph. After the death of his first son, Bell designed a "vacuum jacket," an early but unsuccessful version of the iron lung. In 1881, Alec devised two electrical instruments to help doctors locate an assassin's bullet that was threatening President James A. Garfield's life. But the bullet was

With Mabel's portrait of a great white owl on the wall behind
them, Bell (right) and Thomas Watson confer in Bell's
Boston laboratory. Painting by W. A. Rogers.

. . . . .

too deep for the instruments to be effective and Garfield died
from infection. The following year, in 1882, the Scottish-born
Bell became an American citizen.

Above all, Bell considered his work with the deaf to be of
primary importance. He taught speech to the deaf, demonstrated Visible Speech, founded a day school for the deaf in
Washington, lectured to teachers of the deaf and researched the
hereditary causes of deafness. Toward the end of his life, Bell
commented that "recognition of my work for and interest in the

The Bell family strikes a formal pose in 1885:
Elsie, Mabel, Daisy, and Aleck (left to right).

· · · · ·

education of the deaf has always been more pleasing to me than even recognition of my work with the telephone." Bell's ties to speech and sound were so close, that the word "decibel," which is used for a unit of measuring sound, is a combination of the Latin prefix "deci," meaning tenth, and "Bell."

Bell once declared that "It is possible to teach the deaf to hear speech with their eyes." But of course for the deaf-blind, that wasn't possible. In 1876, Bell met Laura Bridgman, a forty-six-year-old deaf-blind woman whose mind had been opened to the world around her by Samuel Gridley Howe, director of the Perkins Institution for the Blind. It was at a memorial service for Howe that Bell had "quite a little talk" with Laura Bridgman through the one-hand manual alphabet, a system by which the listener cups her hand gently over the speaker's hand as the speaker spells out the letters of the alphabet. "The whole scene was one I shall long remember," Bell commented about their conversation.

And remember it he did. Ten years later, in the summer of 1886, Bell met six-year-old deaf-blind Helen Keller and recalled how much had been done for Laura Bridgman at the Perkins Institution. Realizing immediately what a bright child Helen was, he advised Helen's father to write the Institution's director and request a teacher for his daughter.

The first meeting between Alexander Graham Bell and deaf-blind Helen Keller was a happy coming-together of two remarkable human beings. Some fifteen years later, Helen Keller recalled what that meeting had meant to her: "Child as I was, I at once felt the tenderness and sympathy which endeared Dr. Bell to so many hearts . . . But I did not dream that that interview would be the door through which I should pass from darkness into light, from isolation to friendship, companionship, knowledge, love."

CHAPTER 3

BORN ON June 27, 1880, in Tuscumbia, Alabama, Helen Adams Keller was able to say a word or two by the time she was only six months old. But at the age of nineteen months, she was struck by an "illness which closed my eyes and ears and plunged me into the unconsciousness of a new-born baby." When she recovered from what the doctor called "acute congestion of the stomach and brain," Helen was both deaf and blind, and because she couldn't hear, as the months went by, she lost her ability to speak.

At least her illness hadn't affected her quick mind, and Helen devised some sixty signs to make her wants known. A pull meant come and a push meant go. Pinching a tiny bit of skin on her hand meant small and spreading her fingers wide and bringing her hands together meant large. If she wanted bread, she acted out cutting off slices and buttering them, and if she wanted ice cream, she pretended to work the ice cream freezer and shivered as if she were cold.

By the time she was five, Helen could fold laundry, run errands for her mother upstairs and down, help in the kitchen, feed the hens and turkeys and get into mischief with the servants' children. But along with Helen's increasing ability to make her wants known came a growing frustration and anger.

"I felt as if invisible hands were holding me, and I made frantic efforts to free myself. I struggled—not that struggling helped matters, but the spirit of resistance was strong within me," she admitted later. She also came to understand that other people communicated with their mouths and although she, too, moved her lips, nothing happened. "This made me so angry at times that I kicked and screamed until I was exhausted," she recalled.

Heartsick at their daughter's misery and rage, the Kellers tolerated Helen's violent temper tantrums without making any demands or disciplining her in any way. She ate with her fingers from both her own and other people's plates, shoved aside any object that was in her way, kicked her nurse when she was angry and pinched her grandmother, whom she disliked. When Helen found her newborn sister in a favorite doll's cradle, she tipped the baby out in a jealous fury. At the age of six, she locked her mother in the pantry and then sat on the back porch for three hours gleefully enjoying the jarring vibrations of her mother's pounding on the pantry door. (A servant finally happened by and let Mrs. Keller out.)

The pantry incident was the last straw for the Kellers, who realized that they had to get help for Helen in one form or another. Because their first thought was to find medical treatment, Helen's father and aunt took her to see a well-known eye doctor in Baltimore. Although the doctor could do nothing for Helen, he recommended that she be taken to Washington, D.C., to meet with Alexander Graham Bell for advice on how she could best be educated. It was that meeting with Bell that ultimately unlocked the doors to what Helen called her "triple dungeon."

At Bell's suggestion, Captain Keller wrote to Michael Anagnos, Director of the Perkins Institution for the Blind, requesting a private teacher for Helen. Anagnos immediately thought of his star pupil who had just graduated from Perkins, feisty, headstrong Annie Sullivan.

Partially blind herself, Anne Mansfield Sullivan had been born in 1866 in Massachusetts, the daughter of desperately poor Irish immigrants. After the death of her mother, followed by

Annie Sullivan is only twenty-one when she arrives
at the Keller home in 1887 to become
Helen's teacher and companion.

• • • • •

several years of caring for her drunkard father, Annie and her younger brother were sent to the snake pit that was the state poorhouse in Tewksbury, Massachusetts. Fifty years later, Annie still remembered the death of her beloved brother at Tewksbury, where death was an everyday occurrence. "I sat down between my bed and his empty bed, and I hoped desperately to die. I believe very few children have ever been so completely left alone as I was." But Annie was a survivor. Not only did she survive her four and a half years at Tewksbury, but at the age of fourteen she also talked her way into being accepted as a ward of the state at the Perkins Institution for the Blind. Six years later, in 1886, "Miss Spitfire," as Annie was called, graduated at the head of her class.

Although Annie accepted Captain Keller's offer to teach Helen, she didn't arrive at the Kellers' home in Tuscumbia until the following year. In the meantime, she returned to Perkins to study methods of teaching the deaf-blind, especially the methods used with deaf-blind Laura Bridgman, who still lived at Perkins. (Annie already knew the manual alphabet, having learned it as a student at Perkins.)

Helen Keller always called March 3, 1887, the day that twenty-one year-old Annie Sullivan arrived in Tuscumbia, her "soul's birthday." (It also happened to be Alexander Graham Bell's fortieth birthday.) "The most important day I remember in all my life is the one on which my teacher, Anne Mansfield Sullivan, came to me," she wrote in her autobiography. "I was caught up and held close in the arms of her who had come to reveal all things to me, and, more than all things else, to love me."

But that love came only after a fierce battle between strong-willed Helen Keller and equally strong-willed Annie Sullivan. The simplest chore, such as getting Helen to comb her hair or button her shoes, became a physical contest. Annie refused to let Helen eat from anyone else's plate, made her sit down at the table for meals and eat properly with a spoon. And Helen wasn't allowed to leave the table until she had folded her napkin. Outraged, Helen kicked and slapped Annie, threw herself on the floor screaming and turned every meal into an ordeal. Because the Kellers couldn't bear to see their child in such a state, they sided with Helen against Annie. Finally Annie insisted that she and Helen move to a cottage on the property where the two of them could live and work without family interference.

From the day she arrived, Annie spelled words into Helen's hand, *doll, cake, toy, dog, baby*. Although Helen repeated the words back into Annie's hand, she didn't connect the word that she was spelling with the object. It wasn't until Annie had worked with Helen for a month that "the mystery of language was revealed to me," as Helen later described the dramatic moment.

During a visit to the well house one morning, Annie pumped water over Helen's hand while spelling the word *water* into her other hand. Water! Helen was stunned. Everything had a name and *water* was the name for what was gushing out of the pump. "That living word awakened my soul, gave it light, hope, joy, set it free!" Helen pointed to Annie Sullivan with a questioning look. "Teacher," Annie spelled out and for the rest of their lives together, Helen knew Annie Sullivan as Teacher.

There was no stopping Helen from then on. She insisted that Teacher spell out words for her from the moment they awoke until they went to bed at night. For the next two years, Annie taught Helen the meaning of words, not by drills in a classroom, but by playing hide-and-seek, caring for a litter of puppies, taking walks in the woods, sitting on the banks of the Tennessee River. "For a long time I had no regular lessons . . . everything that could hum, or buzz, or sing, or bloom, had a part in my education," Helen wrote about Annie's methods. "Whenever anything delighted or interested me she talked it over with me."

And Teacher had the good sense to know that Helen needed time alone, too. Much like young Aleck Bell climbing the hills of Edinburgh to dream and watch the gulls, Helen often climbed the mimosa tree in the Kellers' yard. "I spent many happy hours in my tree of paradise, thinking fair thoughts and dreaming bright dreams," she recalled.

Eight-year-old Helen and Annie Sullivan talk with their fingers, 1888.
· · · · ·

Convinced that Helen could best learn as an infant learns, Teacher finger-spelled whole sentences into Helen's hand without explaining every new word, allowing Helen to reason out the meaning for herself. And because Helen was so eager to learn and so enthusiastic about the new world that she was discovering, her basic loving character emerged. "She is naturally a very sweet, affectionate and generous child," Annie wrote to a friend.

Within four or five months of Teacher's arrival, Helen had learned the manual alphabet and could read both Braille and raised letters. Teacher gave her books to read even though she was only able to piece out a few words here and there. And she not only learned to read but write as well. One of Helen's first letters was to Alexander Graham Bell. In November of 1887, she began a correspondence with Bell that would continue for the next thirty-five years. "Dear Dr. Bell, I am glad to write you a letter. Father will send you picture. I and Father and aunt did go to see you in Washington. I did play with your watch. I do love you . . . Good-by, HELEN KELLER."

Soon Helen was turning out letters almost daily. As the months went by, some of the people to whom she wrote were so impressed that they allowed newspapers and magazines to publish her letters, much to the Kellers' dismay. (Only the fact that Bell had been responsible for bringing Annie Sullivan and Helen together prevented the Kellers from criticizing Bell when he, too, turned over a photograph of Helen and one of her letters to a scientific magazine.) Although the Kellers hated any kind of publicity, reporters even began showing up at their Tuscumbia home. By early 1888, when a description of Helen's progress was published in a Perkins Institution report, the words "miracle" and "miracle worker" were being used.

One person, however, never used the word "miracle" and that person was Alexander Graham Bell. "Helen's remarkable achievements are as much due to the genius of her teacher, as to her own brilliant mind," he declared. Bell praised how Teacher read, read, read to Helen, how the learning process went on from morning until night, how Teacher used everyday

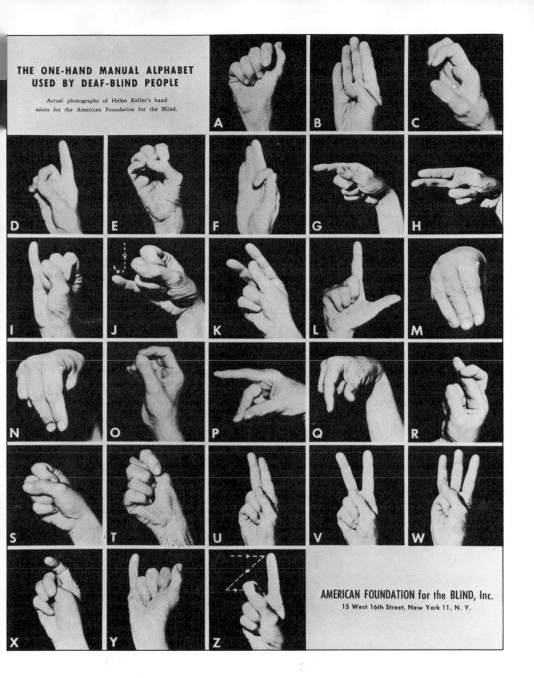

Helen Keller demonstrates the one-hand manual alphabet.

• • • • •

events to teach Helen words and concepts, how she spelled ordinary English into Helen's hand without stopping to explain each new word. Certainly both Bell and Annie Sullivan believed that books held the secret to learning, whether or not every word could be understood. "I would have a deaf child read books in order to learn the language, instead of learning the language in order to read books," Bell commented.

Miracle or not, within a year of Teacher's arrival at the Kellers', Helen was famous throughout the country. And she had come to her fame by the same route that Alexander Graham Bell had arrived at his, by a sense of purpose and enthusiasm for the task at hand, matched with an imaginative and creative mind. Although Helen Keller had broken through her barrier of silence to her "soul's sudden awakening" just as Bell had broken through the world's silence with his invention of the telephone, Helen's struggle to be accepted as a person in her own right was only just beginning.

Because Bell's greatest achievement, and what he would always be known for, had come to him when he was only twenty-nine, Bell, too, was engaged in a struggle. Three years after he had invented the telephone, he wrote: "I can't bear to hear that even my friends should think that I stumbled upon an invention and that there is no more good in me." Like Helen, Bell had to rethink his priorities and focus on new goals for the years ahead.

CHAPTER 4

. . . . .

IN MAY OF 1888, Helen Keller was once again in Washington, D.C., this time to see both Alexander Graham Bell *and* President Grover Cleveland. "We went to see Mr. Cleveland. He lives in a very large and beautiful white house, and there are lovely flowers and many trees and much fresh and green grass around," was Helen's description of her White House experience.

Visiting with Alexander Graham Bell was much more fun. Because the Bells' daughter Daisy was just Helen's age, Bell knew exactly what appealed to a not-quite-eight-year-old child. "Mr. Bell came to see us," Helen reported. "He talked very fast with his fingers about lions and tigers and elephants. He was very kind to send me a fine elephant [toy] . . . When wild animals hunt the elephant he is very angry and he strikes them with his tusks."

Bell also showed Helen the "glove" he had devised. All the letters of the alphabet, as well as the numbers from 1 to 10, were embroidered on the fingers and palm so that words could be spelled out by touching the letters like the keys on a typewriter. But because Annie Sullivan was unenthusiastic about the glove, she never used it with Helen.

At the time of Helen's Washington visit, Bell was very involved with his new research center on deafness that he called the Volta Bureau. The year before, in 1887, he had appointed John Hitz to be the Bureau's superintendent in charge of all information, reports and research papers on the deaf. Today, the Volta Bureau, now called the Alexander Graham Bell Association for the Deaf, is an internationally famous resource center for the education of the deaf . . . Bell's lifelong dream fulfilled.

Helen, Teacher and Mrs. Keller were stopping only briefly in Washington on their way to the Perkins Institution for the Blind in Boston during that spring of 1888. As guests of the Perkins director, Michael Anagnos, Helen and Teacher had been invited to live and study at Perkins. Thrilled to be in classes with other "little blind children," Helen's quick mind soaked up geography, zoology, botany, French and a smattering of Greek, Latin and German. Arithmetic was her least favorite subject. "Arithmetic and I have never been very good friends," she admitted. (Arithmetic and young Aleck Bell had never been very good friends, either.) At least books and Helen were good friends. "Books are the eyes of the blind," she announced.

Books weren't Helen's only passion. She had a passion for people, too. In the years before Teacher came, Helen's strong-willed energy had been trapped inside her, making her lash out at everyone and everything in frustration and anger. But when Helen's mind had been opened by Teacher, that same energy was released to flow outwardly toward others. "Behold, all things are changed! The wild little creature of two weeks ago has been transformed into a gentle child," a delighted Teacher commented less than a month after arriving in Tuscumbia.

While at Perkins, Helen heard about a motherless deaf-blind boy, Tommy Stringer, who was about to be placed in a Pennsylvania poorhouse. "I know what it is to be in darkness," nine-year-old Helen observed, and with that, she appealed to everyone she knew for contributions to bring Tommy to Perkins. "I tell all of my friends about the dear little fellow, because I am sure they will want to bring light and music into his sad life," she said. With Bell's encouragement, Helen succeeded in

Helen happily settles into a routine of study at the
Perkins School for the Blind.

• • • • •

raising some $1,600, enough money to educate the five-year-old Tommy at Perkins for two years.

Certainly Helen had plenty of friends to call on. Although the young Aleck Bell had quite charmed the Bostonians he had met, Helen Keller captivated the entire city. New England's intellectuals, Dr. Edward Everett Hale, Bishop Phillips Brooks and the poets Oliver Wendell Holmes and John Greenleaf Whittier were all enchanted by her loving and generous nature.

During Helen's three years at Perkins, Bell was increasingly drawn to the idea of manned flight, no doubt recalling his boyhood days lying on the Scottish hillsides watching the gulls soar overhead. "The more I experiment, the more convinced I become that flying machines are practical," he declared. And experiment he did, with little monoplanes, primitive helicopter rotors and gunpowder rockets.

At the same time, his work with the deaf flourished. "He is never quite so happy as when he has a little deaf child in his arms," Helen once remarked. It was true. In 1890, Bell founded the American Association for the Promotion of the Teaching of Speech to the Deaf, usually shortened (somewhat) to AAPTSD, or simply the Association.

Believing that communication between people was at the heart of life, Bell preferred the oral method of teaching speech to the deaf. The oral method, which required both lipreading (called speechreading) and speaking (called articulation), was far more difficult to learn than sign language. But above all else, Bell wanted the deaf to be accepted as members of the human family, and he felt that sign language not only isolated the deaf, but also lacked the full richness of the English language. It is a tribute to Bell's efforts that when he founded the Association in 1890, about 40 percent of all deaf people were being taught speech. By the time of his death in 1922, that figure had risen to 80 percent. Nevertheless, the controversy between those who champion lipreading and speech, and those who advocate sign language, has continued to this day.

Over the years, Bell worked with hundreds of deaf children who longed to be able to speak. "One of the greatest achieve-

Tommy Stringer (lower right) and two other deaf-blind children
benefit from Helen's (top left) loving concern.

· · · · ·

ments in the world is that of the child born deaf who learns to talk," he said. Because both his wife and mother were deaf, Bell knew firsthand how important speech was to the deaf. (When she was well over sixty, Bell's mother inquired about the possibility of being taught to lip-read. "Do you think I could learn so late in the day?" she asked her son.) Although Bell's wife Mabel had mastered both lipreading and articulation at an early age, strangers often had trouble understanding her. As far as Bell was concerned, what counted was that Mabel's speech could be understood by family and friends, "not its perfection."

Helen Keller had learned every means of communication available to her, including tapping out messages in Morse code with her feet and receiving replies by feeling the vibrations in the floor. Nevertheless, actual speech was ever on her mind. "The impulse to utter audible sounds had always been strong within me," she wrote in her autobiography. Although Bell had urged Helen's father to allow Annie Sullivan to learn speech-teaching methods at a school for the deaf, Captain Keller had never agreed to it. But when Helen was not quite ten, she *demanded* speech lessons. In the spring of 1890, she began working with Sarah Fuller, principal of the Horace Mann School for the Deaf, formerly the Boston School for Deaf Mutes, where Bell had taught under Sarah Fuller as a young man. (Bell had kept in touch with the school over the years by faithfully sending money to buy clothes and supplies for the students.)

Miss Fuller, after giving Helen eleven lessons, commented: "She was an ideal pupil for she followed every direction with the utmost care, and seemed never to forget anything told her." Helen was thrilled with her newfound ability to articulate words. "I am not dumb now," she declared triumphantly.

But only Sarah Fuller, Teacher and those close to Helen could understand her. Her speech tended either to sound sing-songy when she read out loud, or to lack expression, particularly when she raised her voice. Much like a small child first attempting to read, Helen pronounced each word separately and deliberately. And the inflections and emphasis that give variety to a hearing person's speech were always missing.

Helen's failure to speak well was a lifelong frustration. "I swallowed the very words I especially wanted my listeners to hear. I pushed and strained, I pounded. I defeated myself with too much effort. I committed every sin against the dignity and grace of speech," Helen lamented as an adult. "Learning to speak was the hardest job I ever had, and, alas, I have never quite succeeded."

In 1891, Bell's Volta Bureau published a handsome book called the *Helen Keller Souvenir* for the membership of the Association. Aware of Helen's interest in the handicapped, Bell was sure that she would approve of his publicizing her progress on the chance that it might help others. Furthermore, because Helen was studying at the Perkins Institution for the Blind, Bell realized that she was linked with the cause of the blind. And Bell, as always, was concerned with the deaf. "The public have already become interested in Helen Keller and through her, may perhaps be led to take an interest in the more general subject of the Education of the Deaf," he observed.

Suddenly, in 1891, when everything had been going well for Helen at Perkins, the *Frost King* affair exploded and Helen's life was turned upside down. Helen, who had developed into an enthusiastic writer, had composed a short story which she titled *The Frost King* as a birthday gift for Michael Anagnos, Director of the Perkins Institution. Delighted with Helen's efforts, Anagnos had allowed the story to be published. Almost immediately, a sharp-eyed reader noticed a close resemblance between Helen's *The Frost King* and a story written some twenty years earlier called *Frost Fairies*.

Word spread of the striking similarity between the two. Helen Keller must have copied the original! A fraud, Helen Keller was a fraud! During the worst of the scandal, eleven-year-old Helen jotted down her reaction, and Teacher's, in her diary: "It made us feel so bad to think that people thought we had been untrue and wicked. My heart was full of tears, for I love the beautiful truth with my whole heart and mind."

Anagnos, whose reputation as director of Perkins was also at stake, appointed a board of inquiry. With Teacher dismissed from the room, eight adults questioned a frightened Helen for

Helen and Michael Anagnos, Director of the Perkins
School for the Blind, were on friendly terms
until the Frost King Affair.

• • • • •

two hours as to whether she or Teacher had intentionally cheated. "As I lay in my bed that night, I wept as I hope few children have wept," Helen recalled. "I felt so cold, I imagined I should die before morning, and the thought comforted me."

A furious Mark Twain later described the court of inquiry as "a collection of decayed human turnips" and "solemn donkeys." An even more outraged Bell immediately sent Superintendent of the Volta Bureau John Hitz to Boston to look into the matter. Hitz, who soon became Helen's and Teacher's good friend, as well as converting Helen to his religion of Swedenborgianism, prepared a report that cleared both Helen and Teacher. Helen, blessed with an incredible memory, had heard the original story some three years earlier and although neither she nor Teacher remembered the book, it had apparently registered in Helen's mind without her even realizing it.

With the strength of his name behind it, Bell published Hitz's report, which promptly silenced the criticism and gossip once and for all. As usual, Bell saw beyond the immediate situation to point out how books and reading were the key to Helen's education. The *Frost King* affair, he declared, "will throw light on the manner in which Helen has acquired her marvelous knowledge of language—and do much good."

But Helen was devastated. "Joy deserted my heart, and for a long, long, time I lived in doubt, anxiety and fear," she mourned. "I think if this sorrow had come to me when I was older, it would have broken my spirit beyond repairing."

Because getting through each day locked in her prison of silence and darkness was difficult enough, Helen always made an effort to be positive and optimistic, blocking out any unpleasantness that might make life any harder for her than it already was. The *Frost King* unpleasantness, however, couldn't be blocked out and she became deeply depressed. She was afraid to write for fear that she might copy someone else's material without realizing it, and afraid to read on the chance that she might retain the words and repeat them at some future date. "The thought that what I wrote might not be absolutely my own tormented me," Helen confessed.

Luckily for Helen, Bell traveled to Boston on and off for more than two months during the spring and summer of 1892 defending his telephone patents in court (successfully). He, Helen and Teacher met often. "We saw a great deal of Dr. Bell in those days," Helen recalled. "When the session in court was over, he would come for us, or we would go over to the Bellevue Hotel and wait for him. He was very fond of the theater and of music, and it was never difficult to persuade him to take us to a play or concert." Helen continued: "We took many drives in and around Boston. Often we went to the shore, and if we could find an old sailor to take us out in his boat, Dr. Bell was the happiest man alive."

Bell, Helen and Teacher not only visited back and forth, but Bell also gave Helen a speech lesson. (She begged for more.) As an adult, Helen reflected on the meaning of friendships: "Friends create the world anew each day. Without their loving care, courage would not suffice to keep hearts strong for life." Certainly during that painful spring of 1892, Alexander Graham Bell's friendship and support did much to keep the twelve-year-old Helen's heart strong for life.

. . . . .

CHAPTER 5

"I HAVE NEVER met anyone who knew Dr. Bell personally who did not feel that he had made a lasting impression upon his or her life," Helen Keller once said. Certainly Bell made a lasting impression on Helen's life . . . and Annie Sullivan's, too. Years after Bell's death, Annie Sullivan was asked how she had kept going at such a difficult task for so long. She replied that, besides her love for Helen, "I think it must have been Dr. Bell—his faith in me." The admiration was mutual. Bell praised Annie as one of the great teachers of her time, writing to her of his respect. "The principles that guided you in the early education of Helen are of the greatest importance to all teachers of the deaf."

Because Annie Sullivan was Helen's lifeline to the world, she was also Helen's source of information, communication and love. "Teacher seems a part of myself," Helen acknowledged as a teenager. A few years later, she said, "My teacher is so near to me that I scarcely think of myself apart from her."

The relationship went both ways. As a child, Annie had lost the only two people she had ever loved, her mother and her brother. Now she had Helen. "I have found a real friend—one who will never get away from me, or try to, or want to," she wrote soon after arriving in Tuscumbia at the age of twenty-one.

Others recognized Helen and Teacher's mutual dependence, too. Mark Twain pointed out that ". . . it took the pair of you to make a complete and perfect whole." The famous educator Dr. Maria Montessori remarked to Helen: "She [Teacher] is the creator of a soul, but you had the soul to be created." Certainly the two were inseparable.

In June of 1892, Helen and Teacher traveled back to Tuscumbia, with Helen still depressed over the *Frost King* affair. But in the fall, she was given a new typewriter and at last she began writing again, this time the story of her early years for a children's magazine.

During that same fall, a formally dressed Alexander Graham Bell opened the New York to Chicago telephone line at the A.T. and T. offices amidst great fanfare and publicity. And then, in the spring of 1893, the worlds of Helen Keller and Alexander Graham Bell came together for a happy occasion.

The Volta Bureau had long since outgrown its original quarters in an empty stable behind Melville and Eliza Bell's Washington home. (Bell's parents had moved from Canada to Washington in 1881 to be near their only son and his family.) On May 8, 1893, Helen turned over the first shovelful of dirt for the foundation of the new Volta Bureau library that would rise across the street from the old stable. "Full of joy I turned the first sod with my teacher on one side and Alexander Graham Bell and John Hitz on the other," Helen reported. (The handsome yellow brick and sandstone building is now headquarters for the Alexander Graham Bell Association for the Deaf.)

And Captain Keller permitted Helen and Teacher to visit the Rochester School for the Deaf with Bell during the spring of 1893. Helen, as always, was an immediate hit. Like any twelve-year-old, Helen loved riddles. Spelling into Bell's hand one night at supper, she asked the Rochester faculty and students what word was formed by these three clues: "My first is a body of water. My second is an exclamation; my third is used in fishing." When no one could come up with the answer, Helen triumphantly spelled the solution into Bell's hand. "Bay-O-Net," he repeated to the audience.

Bell is in the spotlight as he opens the telephone line
between New York and Chicago, 1892.

• • • • •

At the ground-breaking ceremony for the new Volta Bureau, Helen Keller (holding shovel) is surrounded by the Bell family and other friends, 1893.

· · · · ·

While in Rochester, Helen and Bell plotted an adventure. "Mr. Bell and I planned it together, and Mr. Bell made all the arrangements before we told teacher anything about it," Helen wrote her mother in great excitement. "This was the surprise—I was to have the pleasure of taking my dear teacher to see Niagara Falls! Wasn't it splendid! Mr. Bell is always so kind and thoughtful!" Although Bell wasn't able to accompany them, he gave Helen a down pillow and told her that if she held it against herself, she would better be able to feel the vibrations of the Falls.

The trip turned out to be a great success. "The hotel was so near the river that I could feel it rushing past by putting my hand on the window," Helen marveled. And Helen was fearless. She descended 120 feet in an elevator to experience the churning of the "violent eddies and whirlpools" in the gorge below the Falls. She and Teacher then crossed from the United States to Canada over an 800-foot-long bridge that was suspended more than 250 feet above the water. She related the sensation. "It is difficult to describe my emotions when I stood on the point which overhangs the American Falls and felt the air vibrate and the earth tremble."

In June of 1893, Helen and Teacher were once again in Washington for a visit with the Bells and their daughters, fifteen-year-old Elsie and thirteen-year-old Daisy. Helen, it seemed, was as fearless as ever. Daisy, who was just Helen's age, wrote to Helen some years later: "Once—when you were staying with us in Washington . . . I took you up on the roof of Grandmama Hubbard's carriage house . . . I was very much surprised to be soundly scolded for taking such chances with you—But there never seemed to be anything you weren't willing and able to do."

Elsie remembered the incident, too. "Oh, we got an awful scolding for doing that—taking Helen up a ladder onto the roof! But Helen certainly had a good time!" As an adult, Helen fondly recalled her good times with the Bell girls: "Elsie and Daisy were always ready to play with me, and Daisy tried to spell into my hand all the bright things she heard so that I could laugh with her."

During that same visit, Bell invited the Washington Literary Society to his home to meet Helen, hear her recite poetry (and her newest riddles) and listen to a report on Annie Sullivan's teaching methods. Although the evening probably wasn't half the fun for Helen that her earlier adventure on the carriage house roof had been, Bell's guests were charmed. "Washington has just had a visit from wonderful Helen Keller who has been the guest, much petted and loved, of Professor Graham Bell," reported a Washington newspaper.

By now Helen was as much of an international celebrity as

Niagara Falls provides a dramatic backdrop for
Helen Keller (right) and Annie Sullivan, 1893.

· · · · ·

Bell. When Bell escorted Helen and Teacher to the Chicago World's Fair in the summer of 1893 following their Washington visit, Helen attracted as much attention as either Bell or the Fair itself.

For three weeks, Bell was the perfect host. "Dr. Bell went everywhere with us and in his delightful way described to me the objects of greatest interest," Helen wrote. "Dr. Bell went with us himself to the electrical building and showed us some of the historical telephones." And Helen had special permission to handle the exhibits, everything from valuable French bronzes to Tiffany diamonds to ancient Mexican relics, although she confessed that she "shrank from touching" the Egyptian mummies. "I took in the glories of the Fair with my fingers," she said.

The world had always come to Helen through her fingers and hands. The clasp of a hand could reveal love, anger, fear, sorrow. "My hand is to me what your hearing and sight together are to you . . . It is the hand that binds me to the world of men and women," Helen explained. "If I had made a man, I should certainly have put the brain and soul in his finger-tips."

Because Bell's concern for deaf causes was never far from his mind, he had planned the trip to Chicago with Helen and Teacher to take place at the same time as the third annual meeting of the Association to Promote the Teaching of Speech to the Deaf that was also being held at the Fair. As president, he introduced Helen to teachers of the deaf, who agreed that they "saw and heard enough to remove all their doubts." But always being in the limelight had its drawbacks for Helen, who was, after all, only thirteen. "Is anybody watching us?" she asked a young teacher with whom she was spending the day. When the answer was no, Helen cried, "Then let's romp."

The following year, in June of 1894, Bell invited Helen and Teacher to the fourth annual meeting of the Association in Chautauqua, New York. (For the occasion, a thoughtful Mrs. Bell bought new clothes for both Helen and Teacher.) But Teacher was concerned that the meeting would involve too much "speechmaking and handshaking" for Helen's good. "I hope if we do go, Mr. Bell will see that the dear child is protected as much as possible," she worried.

Actually Helen thrived on being with people and wasn't shy in the least at finding herself in new situations. "I am myself a sociable creature. I like parties and companionship," she announced. Perhaps Teacher's reluctance stemmed from her own fears. She confessed that she had always dreaded social functions and meeting people. Bell seemed to be the exception. "I never felt at ease with anyone until I met him," she revealed. "Dr. Bell had a happy way of making people feel pleased with themselves."

To add to Teacher's nervousness, Bell had asked her to give a speech on her educational methods to the Association membership. Because Teacher dreaded giving speeches even more than she dreaded meeting people, Bell, in the end, had to read her speech for her. Entitled "The Instruction of Helen Keller," Teacher's theme was that in the early years, a child's natural curiosity should guide learning and that all learning should be enjoyable. And like Bell, Teacher believed that books opened the door to learning. "Children should be encouraged to read for the pure delight of it," she advised.

As soon as Association business was finished, it was vacation time for everyone and the Bells invited Helen and Teacher to their new summer home near Baddeck in the Canadian province of Nova Scotia. The Bells had first visited Baddeck nine years before and fallen in love with what Mabel Bell described as its "forest-covered hills, undulating valleys with trim, well-kept fields and neat little houses, pretty streams."

Gradually, the Bells had bought up hundreds of acres of land on a point high above Bras d'Or Lake that reminded Bell of his beloved Scottish homeland. The huge house that the Bells had built on the point was called Beinn Bhreagh (pronounced Ben Vree-ah), which was Scottish Gaelic for "Beautiful Mountain." Described by a Canadian newspaper as "The Bell Palace at Baddeck," the house, with its towers, porches, wings, gables, dormers, balconies and twelve fireplaces, at least qualified as a mansion, if not a palace.

Bell and fourteen-year-old Helen are joined by Annie Sullivan in
a hand-talk during a meeting for teachers of the deaf, 1894.

• • • • •

For the rest of their lives together, the Bells lived at Beinn Bhreagh from early spring until November to escape the Washington heat, which still gave Bell bad headaches. Bell also felt the need to escape the Washington social scene, to be alone with his family and to work in seclusion. If the big house became too crowded, Bell would retreat to his houseboat, *Mabel of Beinn Bhreagh,* which was anchored in a nearby cove.

Bell's son-in-law once said, "Mr. Bell led a peculiarly isolated life; I have never known anyone who spent so much of his time alone." Bell didn't even want to be bothered by the ring of a telephone. When a visitor to his Washington home asked to use the telephone, Bell replied: "There is a telephone in the house but the pesky thing is as far from here as I could possibly get it." (To the end of his days, Bell answered the telephone with "Hoy! Hoy!" instead of the more popular "Hello.")

Although Bell had received honors around the world, and belonged to more clubs and organizations than he probably could have named, he was essentially a very private person. In 1890, Bell wrote to Mabel, "I feel more and more as I grow older the tendency to retire into myself and be alone with my thoughts." Fortunately, Mabel, who continually urged Bell to move out into the world, refused to let him withdraw. "Please try to come out of your hermit cell," she scolded one time when they were separated. "Accept all the invitations to dinner you get," she suggested during another separation.

Working through most of the night, and then sleeping through most of the morning, reinforced Bell's sense of solitude. It was a routine that Bell continued right up to the end of his life. During one of his trips to Japan, he was to have been received by the Emperor of Japan at 10 A.M. Bell's servant roused him early, saw that he was properly dressed and sent him off. As soon as Bell returned, he went straight to bed and slept until 2 P.M. Upon awakening, he inquired as to when he was to meet the Emperor!

When Helen and Teacher visited Beinn Bhreagh in July of 1894, solitude was the last thing on Bell's, or anyone else's, mind. On July 19th, Bell hosted a spectacular celebration for his

Sheep graze on the back lawn of the Bells' summer home at Beinn Bhreagh.

· · · · ·

parents' fiftieth wedding anniversary. With bonfires blazing and the trees strung with Chinese lanterns, two hundred guests, including Helen and Teacher, were entertained by a military band and a dazzling display of fireworks. Helen described her vacation at Beinn Bhreagh as "one of the happiest visits of my life."

That fall, October 1894, Bell's dream for Helen to attend a school for the deaf became a reality when Captain Keller allowed Helen to enroll at the Wright-Humanson School for the Deaf in New York City. Accompanied by Annie Sullivan, Helen was to study speech and lipreading, as well as take singing lessons to strengthen her voice. (As the only deaf-blind student, lipreading for Helen meant placing her fingers on the speaker's lips in order to "read" what was being said.)

After two years at Wright-Humanson, Helen's speech improved, but not as much as she had anticipated. "My progress in lip-reading and speech was not what my teachers and I had hoped and expected it would be," she acknowledged. On the other hand, she had made new friends, toured New York City, learned to ride horseback, bobsledded in Central Park and was considered to be full of fun by the other students.

Always a goal setter, in 1896, when Helen was sixteen, she zeroed in on a new goal. She announced that she wanted to go to college with seeing and hearing girls. "The thought of going to college took root in my heart and became an earnest desire," she declared. And Helen was nothing if not determined. "It seems sometimes as if I could never accomplish all I wish to," she wrote to a friend. "But I am going to think *I can;* for I know patience and perseverance always conquer in the end." Although Alexander Graham Bell had been awarded several honorary degrees, and was popularly known as Dr. or Professor Bell, he had never finished college. Now Helen Keller wanted to take that giant step and he couldn't have been more delighted than if he had made the decision himself.

CHAPTER 6

Money MATTERS had never much interested Alexander Graham Bell. "Business is hateful to me at all times," he once admitted. But interested in money matters or not, Bell was aware that Helen's ongoing education was a heavy financial burden for the Kellers, who were not a wealthy family.

In the summer of 1894, Bell wrote to Captain Keller suggesting that a trust fund be set up to help pay for Helen's education, which of necessity included Annie Sullivan's living expenses as well. Although Captain Keller, who had fought in the Civil War and called himself a "gentleman farmer," was a proud man, he replied to Bell: "Your kindness to my dear Child touches me very deeply . . . I am constrained to consent to any plan you have in view for their [Helen and Teacher's] welfare and happiness."

There was no question that Bell meant well, but two years passed before he did anything about putting together a trust fund for Helen. "Dr. Bell is coming here tomorrow to meet several gentlemen and arrange with them about money for my education," Helen wrote to her mother in 1896 during her second year at the Wright-Humanson School in New York.

But only one other person showed up at the meeting and an annoyed Annie Sullivan remarked that "Mr. Bell's visit was most unsatisfactory; for it brought only disappointment and discouragement. Mr. Bell did a great deal of talking which was not to the point, and when it came to doing, he was not in it." Teacher, like the Kellers, had assumed that Bell would head up the fund, but apparently that had never been his intention. Finally, in December of 1896, Eleanor and Lawrence Hutton, a wealthy New York couple who had become friendly with Helen, volunteered to be in charge of the Helen Keller Trust Fund, which would raise money for Helen's education from all over the country through public contributions.

Although Teacher may have been annoyed, it's doubtful if the fund would ever have been launched in the first place if it hadn't been for Bell and the prestige of his name. And Bell was unfailingly generous. He immediately contributed $1,000 to the fund and whenever there was a special occasion, or even when he simply sensed that Helen and Teacher could use extra money, he made sure that they had it.

"It would not surprise me to learn that an understanding friend like Dr. Bell had smoothed the financial thorns out of our way so that we could attend conventions for the deaf," Helen wisely surmised. Certainly if Bell himself didn't pay for Helen and Teacher's expenses to attend Association meetings, he saw to it that the Association did. And Helen's attendance at the fifth annual Association meeting in Philadelphia in July of 1896 was special for both Helen and Bell. For the first time, Bell had arranged to have Helen speak to the entire membership. After two years of speech lessons at the Wright-Humanson School, Helen was anxious to give it a try, despite lingering doubts.

"If you knew all the joy I feel in being able to speak to you to-day, I think you would have some idea of the value of speech to the deaf, and you would understand why I want every little deaf child in all this great world to have an opportunity to learn to speak," Helen told a standing-room-only audience in her still-difficult-to-understand voice. "One can never consent to creep when one feels an impulse to soar."

And Helen had always set her heart on soaring. Now, at the age of sixteen, she decided that the college she wanted to attend was Radcliffe, one of the most demanding colleges in the country. If she could make the grade at Radcliffe, she could make the grade anywhere. "I did not want people to tell me what I should do or not do just because I happened to be different from others. I preferred to compete with seeing and hearing girls," she announced. Later, when Helen was asked why she had chosen such a difficult school, she replied, "Because they didn't want me at Radcliffe, and as I was stubborn by nature, I chose to override their objections."

When Helen, Teacher and Bell were all staying at the Parker House in Boston in July of 1896, Bell told Helen that he was as eager for her to prove herself as she was. "I like to think of Helen fighting her way through Radcliffe College in competition with seeing and hearing young ladies," was Bell's opinion on the subject.

In order to prepare for Radcliffe, Helen entered the Cambridge School for Young Ladies in October of 1896, her first experience with hearing and seeing students. As soon as Helen arrived, the school's headmaster, Arthur Gilman, tested her with an old set of Harvard entrance exams. The results were astounding. Helen passed the Harvard exams in Greek and Roman history, English, German and French!

Because Helen attended classes with hearing and seeing students, Annie Sullivan had to be present at all times in order to spell the lessons into her hand. And because none of the textbooks were in Braille or raised print, Teacher also had to read Helen's daily assignments into her hand. But Teacher's eyes, which had been severely damaged by a childhood disease, suffered from such constant use. Helen voiced her concern in a letter to a friend: "Of course my work is harder than it would be if I could read my lessons over by myself. But it is harder for Teacher than it is for me because the strain on her poor eyes is so great and I cannot help worrying about them."

Nevertheless, classes went well. "Helen is the liveliest and happiest child in the world yet!" Headmaster Gilman commented soon after Helen's arrival. But by the following year, a far less enthusiastic Gilman was accusing Teacher of pushing Helen too hard and overworking her to the point of exhaustion. Gilman wrote Bell six letters during the fall of 1897 expressing alarm over Helen's health and urging that Helen and Teacher be separated for Helen's own good. "Helen has grown beyond

Helen Keller listens to a book by reading Annie Sullivan's lips.

• • • • •

her teacher and needs something quite different. A separation would be a trial for a while, but Helen would recover from it," Gilman recommended to Bell in December of 1897. He made the same suggestion in letters to Mrs. Keller. (Captain Keller had died the year before.)

It wasn't until December 8th that Helen learned what Gilman was up to. "Then, all of a sudden, the most dreadful sorrow burst upon us which we ever endured," she wrote, obviously stunned. "I touched her [Teacher's] trembling hand and at once saw that something terrible had happened. 'What is it, Teacher?' I cried in dismay. 'Helen, I fear we are going to be separated!' 'What! Separated? What do you mean?' I said, utterly bewildered."

To separate the inseparable was unthinkable, not only for Helen, but also for Teacher, who sent frantic telegrams to Mrs. Keller, the Bells and two other friends. Bell, who was on shipboard at the time and unavailable, instructed Volta Bureau superintendent John Hitz to investigate the situation in person, just as he had in the *Frost King* affair. Hitz's seven-page report to Bell urged that Helen and Teacher *not* be separated.

As always, Bell's influence carried a lot of weight and when he strongly advised "that nothing could justify such a course," Mrs. Keller and Helen's other supporters agreed. It was the first and last time that a separation between Helen and Teacher was ever attempted . . . or even considered.

That, of course, ended Helen's studies at the Cambridge School. For the next two years, she worked with a private tutor to prepare for the Radcliffe exams, which she took in June of 1899. Not only did Helen pass the exams, but she also "passed with credit in Advanced Latin." It was a triumphant moment. An elated Bell ordered that an updated *Helen Keller Souvenir* booklet be published which would cover Helen's education from 1892 to 1899. This time the booklet included an article by Helen herself, who was becoming an increasingly gifted writer.

In more ways than one, Helen's acceptance at Radcliffe was as much of a victory for Bell as it was for Helen. During Helen's teen years, Bell had spent much of his time traveling around the

In preparation for Radcliffe College, Helen Keller
studies Braille books, 1899.

· · · · ·

country, lobbying and working for state-supported day schools
for deaf children. Ideally, the schools would be housed in public
schools so that the deaf children could interact and play with
hearing children, as well as return home to their families at
night.

In 1883, Bell had begun his own private day school for the
deaf in Washington. But finding trained teachers had been a
problem, and Bell had been forced to close down the school

after only two years. It had been such a devastating blow that Bell had told his wife Mabel that his whole life had been "shipwrecked." Now Helen Keller had proven that a deaf girl, not only deaf but blind as well, could compete on an equal footing with students who could both hear and see.

Nevertheless, Bell had to step into Helen's life once again, this time after she had already begun her studies at Radcliffe. Even as a young woman, Helen had strongly sympathized with social causes, whether it was helping the handicapped, fighting political injustice or arguing for disarmament during the Spanish-American War. Consequently, she took to heart the suggestion of a friend, Ida Chamberlin, that she use her good name to open a school for deaf-blind children in New York City to be called the Helen Keller Home.

Although Helen wasn't enthusiastic, she was anxious to be useful in the world. Furthermore, because she was already worried that her strenuous Radcliffe program of courses was further weakening Teacher's eyes, she traveled to New York to discuss the project with her friends there. All of them advised her to put aside thoughts of opening a school until she had finished college. "They were very kind," an unconvinced Helen commented, "but I could not help feeling that they spoke more from a business than a humanitarian point of view. I am sure they did not quite understand how passionately I desire that all who are afflicted like myself shall receive their rightful inheritance of thought, knowledge and love."

Bell, who called the plan "a gigantic blunder," settled the matter once and for all. "We had a long talk with Dr. Bell. Finally he proposed a plan which delighted us all beyond words," Helen wrote. "We clapped our hands and shouted." Bell, of course, had always opposed isolating the deaf and blind, whether it was in school or in the work force. Perhaps, he suggested, Ida Chamberlin and her friends could organize an association for the promotion of the education of the deaf and blind, while Teacher could train others to instruct deaf and blind children in their homes just the way she had instructed Helen. In turn, Helen, by going to Radcliffe, could show the world that a deaf-blind person could keep up with hearing and seeing students at a highly competitive college.

It was the perfect solution for everyone. "Aunt Ida went away beaming with pleasure, and Teacher and I felt more light of heart than we had for sometime," Helen rejoiced. Helen's respect for Bell's wisdom was boundless. "He had an extraordinary gift of presenting difficult problems in a simple and vivid manner."

Although she made friends and joined in many of the college activities, her four years at Radcliffe were difficult for Helen, as well as for Teacher . . . and for Radcliffe. Despite Helen's unfailing optimism and good humor, there was often an underlying current of sadness to her college experience. A few months before she finished her course of studies, Helen spoke to a group of Radcliffe graduates. "I have sometimes had a depressing sense of isolation in the midst of my classmates. There are times when one wearies of books," she confessed, "and when one reaches out to the warm, living touch of a friendly hand." At least she could always count on Bell's support. "How closely I felt your sympathy and forward-looking faith in me when I fought my way through college!" Helen wrote to Bell a number of years later.

Teacher, too, was under pressure and her eyes bothered her constantly. She had to attend all of Helen's classes and spell out the lectures as well as any required reading that wasn't in Braille or raised print. As for Radcliffe, the dean later admitted: "Radcliffe did not desire Helen Keller as a student. It was necessary that all instruction should reach her through Miss Sullivan and this necessity presented difficulties."

Difficulties or not, Helen graduated from Radcliffe College Cum Laude (with honor) in June of 1904 with ninety-five other young women. Although Bell was at Beinn Bhreagh and unable to attend the ceremony, dependable John Hitz was in the audience. Guided across the platform by Teacher, Helen received her diploma from the president's hand to the vibrations of polite applause that quickly turned into an ovation. Helen Keller's graduation, reported a Boston newspaper, "is a notable event in the history of American education."

During Helen Keller's second year at Radcliffe, she and Bell
talk by means of the manual alphabet, 1902.
· · · · ·

In 1904 Helen Keller graduates with honors from Radcliffe College.

. . . . .

Helen had fulfilled her own dream as well as the dream that Bell had always had for her, and for the deaf everywhere. She had set goals for herself in the hearing and seeing world and achieved them all. After Bell's death, his daughter Daisy wrote to Helen: "I remember how much Father loved you and how proud he was of you." And well he might have been.

. . . . .

CHAPTER 7

I N 1 8 9 7, B E L L took over the presidency of the National Geographic Society, which his father-in-law, Gardiner Greene Hubbard, had founded nine years earlier. The theme of the Society, Bell announced, would be THE WORLD AND ALL THAT IS IN IT. Bell, who had cared passionately about the world around him ever since his childhood, might just as well have been stating the theme of his own life. Music, scientific experiments, inventing, teaching, public speaking and work with the deaf all fascinated him.

"What a man my husband is!" Mabel Bell had marveled when they were first married. "I am perfectly bewildered at the number and size of the ideas with which his head is crammed." Thomas Watson, Bell's young electrical assistant, remarked about Bell that "his head seemed to be a teeming beehive." In an 1891 speech, Bell declared: "The inventor is a man who looks around upon the world and is not contented with things as they are. He wants to improve whatever he sees, he wants to benefit the world; he is haunted by an idea, the spirit of inventiveness possesses him."

And Bell gave all of himself to whatever project was at hand. "My mind concentrates itself on the subject that happens to occupy it and then all things else in the Universe—including father, mother, wife, children, *life itself,* become for the time being of secondary importance," he admitted.

Bell's range of interests worked both for and against him. Certainly his work on the multiple telegraph, the telephone, the phonograph, aeronautics, the National Geographic Society and teaching speech to the deaf had an enormous impact in the whole field of communication. On the other hand, he never had the single-minded purpose of a Thomas Edison. (They were exactly the same age.) Unlike Edison, Bell seldom saw an idea through to completion, let alone showed any interest in either its patenting or marketing. He once commented: "If my ideas are worth patenting, let others do it. Let others endure the worry, the anxiety, and the expense."

When one project didn't work out, he simply moved on to another. "I do not think I ever saw Dr. Bell discouraged. He was always ready to jest about his experimental misfortunes," Helen Keller observed. And age didn't dim Bell's enthusiasm. Many times over the years he had been heard to exclaim: "Life is extraordinarily interesting!"

Although Helen Keller could never fully participate in the world around her, she had the same kind of eager curiosity and zest for new experiences that Bell had. "The wonderfulness of life and creation grows with each day I live," she exulted. Knowing of Helen's thirst to learn, Bell did far more to further her education than simply donate money to her trust fund. "I have never known another man with Dr. Bell's many sidedness and charm," Helen said. "He could explain the most complicated problems in so simple a way that I could understand them."

Even though Helen was never able to use the telephone without assistance, Bell wanted her to understand what his invention meant to the world . . . and to him. Helen described how Bell had placed her hand on a telephone pole during a walk: "I had never put my hand on a pole before. 'Does it hum like that all the time?' I asked. 'Yes,' he told me, 'all the time. That even singing never stops; for it is singing the story of life, and life never stops.' " After explaining to Helen how voices are carried

Helen Keller appreciates the beauty of a rose through its fragrance.
∙ ∙ ∙ ∙ ∙

Helen Keller and Bell finger-talk as John Hitz (top left)
and a friend look on, August 1901.

• • • • •

over the wires, Bell continued, " 'Those copper wires up there
are carrying the news of birth and death, war and finance,
failure and success, from station to station around the world.
Listen! I fancy I hear laughter, tears, life's vows broken and
mended.' " The story reveals more about Bell than it does about
Helen. To Bell, the telephone was never a mere mechanical
device. Instead, it went to the heart of what he cared about
most, bridging the solitude and loneliness that separate one
human being from another.

Bell's account of the 1866 laying of the telegraph cable under the Atlantic Ocean from Newfoundland to Ireland enchanted Helen. "I was twelve years, and that story of heroism and the wonder of the human imagination, as told by Dr. Bell, thrilled me as a fairy tale thrills other children," she wrote.

And the two friends shared a love for both books and travel. "Snatches of poetry, reminiscences of Scotland, interesting descriptions of Japan, which he had visited some years earlier, flowed through his skilfull fingers into my hand," Helen recalled. "He recited favorite passages from 'In Memoriam,' *The Tempest* and *Julius Caesar*."

But not all was seriousness between them. "Doctor Bell was very fond of animals and we used to go to visit the Zoo together, not only in Washington but in other cities where we were attending meetings," Helen wrote. "I remember how I poked a fierce alligator in the water and how it sulked and struck my stick."

For her fourteenth birthday, Bell gave Helen a bird, a handsome cockatoo, "which I called Jonquil because of his glorious yellow crest. Jonquil was a beauty, but he was a menace armoured in lovely white and gold feathers. He used to perch on my foot as I read, rocking back and forth as I turned the pages. Every now and then he would hop to my shoulder and rub his head against my ear and face, sometimes putting his long, sharp, hooked bill in my mouth, sending ripples of terror down my spine." With Jonquil tyrannizing family and friends alike, the Kellers finally had to give him away.

Bell and Helen kept in touch during Helen's Radcliffe years. "I feel that we are apart when I would like to come close to you, and talk to you face to face, and heart to heart," Bell wrote. So that Helen could read his letters without an interpreter, Bell even learned Braille, although it never came easily to him. Helen brushed aside his apologies. "My dear Dr. Bell; I was perfectly delighted to receive your letter and to be able to read it myself. It seemed almost as if you clasped my hand in yours and spoke to me in the old, dear way," she replied in praise of his efforts.

By this time, Bell was deep into work with the 1900 census

report, putting together statistics on the deaf, a job that took him more than five years. And he was still fascinated with the prospect of manned flight. "I believe that it will be possible in a very few years for a person to take his dinner in New York at 7 or 8 o'clock in the evening and eat his breakfast in either Ireland or England the following morning," Bell predicted, quite accurately.

Because kites required neither a pilot nor an expensive motor, Bell began flying kites in preparation for designing the airplanes themselves. In 1898, Bell told his wife Mabel that ". . . the importance of kite flying as a step to a practical flying machine grows upon me." Bell soon developed tetrahedral kites that consisted of equal-sided triangles banked together to combine strength, lightness and simplicity. In December of 1906, a tetrahedral kite that Bell named the "Frost King" carried a 165-pound man more than thirty feet above the ground for a short distance. By christening his successful kite the "Frost King," Bell at last turned Helen's unhappy *Frost King* affair at Perkins Institution fourteen years earlier into a triumphant moment.

"I suppose," Helen reflected while at Radcliffe, "that Mr. Bell has nothing but kites and flying machines on his tongue's end. Poor dear man, how I wish he would stop wearing himself out in this unprofitable way—at least it seems unprofitable to me." A few years later, when Bell was ailing, Helen wrote: "I do hope kite-flying will make Mr. Bell feel like himself again."

Helen was in a position to know about Bell's kites. On a visit to Beinn Bhreagh in 1901, Helen had experienced kite flying firsthand. "I was there and really helped him fly kites. On one of them I noticed that the strings were of wire, and having had some experience in bead work, I said I thought they would break. Dr. Bell said, 'No!' with great confidence, and the kite was sent up. It began to pull and tug, and lo, the wires broke," she reported, obviously pleased to have been proven right. "After that, he asked me if the strings were all right and changed them at once when I answered in the negative. Altogether we had great fun."

Helen had great fun with Elsie and Daisy Bell, too. Along

Bell works on his tetrahedral forms at Beinn Bhreagh, 1907.

· · · · ·

with Teacher, Helen spent one adventuresome night with Elsie and Daisy on the Bells' houseboat. "When the moon rose," Helen related, "we got down into the lake by means of a rope ladder. There we were, four alone with ourselves and perfection of water and moonlight! The air was quite cold; but the water was deliciously warm, and our joy knew no bounds. Then what a scramble we had up the ladder to see who could get to her blankets first!" ("Who put salt in the water?" had been Helen's reaction to her first swim in the ocean.)

At the time of her visit to Beinn Bhreagh, Helen was a good-looking young woman of twenty-one. A reporter had earlier described her as "a handsome, well-formed, graceful girl . . . Her chief beauty, next to her hands, is the mass of short brown

Although the string isn't visible, Bell and Helen Keller fly a kite together at Beinn Bhreagh in the summer of 1901.

. . . . .

curly hair that falls on her shoulders . . . Her chin is beautifully formed, the mouth and teeth are good, her complexion is clear and healthy and the expression of her face is wonderfully attractive in its bright alertness."

Helen's beauty and the possibility of her marrying some time in the future were on Bell's mind during her 1901 visit. "It seems to me, Helen, a day must come when love which is more than friendship will knock at the door of your heart and demand to be let in," he finger-spelled into her hand. "I often think of your future. To me you are a sweet, desirable young girl, and it is natural to think about love and happiness when we are young." He paused. "Do not think that because you cannot see or hear, you are debarred from the supreme happiness of womanhood."

"Oh, but I am happy, very happy!" Helen protested. "I have my teacher and my mother and you, and all my other friends . . . I really don't care a bit about being married."

But Bell persisted. "You are very young and it's natural that you shouldn't take what I have said seriously now; but I have long wanted to tell you how I felt about your marrying."

To Helen's relief, their conversation was interrupted. "I was glad when Mrs. Bell and Miss Sullivan joined us, and the talk became less personal," she recalled.

When Helen returned to Radcliffe from Beinn Bhreagh in the fall, she thanked Mabel Bell in her usual gracious manner: "The smell of the ocean and the fragrance of the pines have followed me to Cambridge and linger about me like a benediction," she wrote. In addition to their deafness and their mutual affection for Bell, Helen and Mabel had much in common. They were both people-lovers who were happiest when surrounded by family and friends. And they both insisted that deafness was more of a curse than blindness.

"I have always declared I would sooner be blind than deaf," Mabel once said. Helen, who always referred to herself as deaf-blind, rather than blind-deaf, expressed the same opinion over and over. "Deafness is a heavier handicap for me than lack of sight . . . I feel the affliction of deafness far more than blindness . . . Deafness in the young is a much worse misfortune than blindness . . . The problems of deafness are deeper and more complex, if not more important, than those of blindness." A sympathetic Bell agreed with his wife and Helen. "Who can picture the isolation of their lives?" he demanded.

Despite Helen's almost unfailing good spirits and optimism, she occasionally referred to the pain of that isolation. "Sometimes, it is true, a sense of isolation enfolds me like a cold mist as I sit alone and wait at life's shut gate. Beyond there is light and music and sweet companionship. But I may not enter. Fate, silent, pitiless, bars the way," she once wrote.

But Helen never gave in to dark thoughts for long. In 1901, during her first year at Radcliffe, she began her autobiography, to be titled *The Story of My Life*. Although she had been writing since she was a child, and would continue to write for the rest of her life, her style sometimes seemed stiff and stilted. At other times, it was overly sentimental and flowery. But that was only natural. After all, most of Helen's sense of words came from books and not everyday conversation. And when Teacher spoke to Helen through the manual alphabet, she had to shorten and abbreviate what she was spelling out, so that Helen never had a real sense of everyday language. Much as Bell admired Annie Sullivan's teaching methods, he once teased her that she had made Helen "a little old woman."

It was in 1902, the year after Helen started writing her autobiography, that John Macy, a bright young Harvard graduate, came to work for Helen as her secretary. Within a short time, he had learned the manual language, helped Helen work on her autobiography, acted as her agent with her publisher . . . and by 1905, he had become engaged to Annie Sullivan.

Soon after Annie Sullivan accepted John's proposal, she and Helen traveled to Washington to tell Bell of the upcoming marriage. Bell's feelings were mixed. He was happy for Teacher but worried about Helen. "Are you going to take my advice now and build your own nest?" he asked her. "No," she replied. "I know I have nothing to give a man that would make up for such an unnatural burden." Bell continued to press her. "You will change your mind some day, young woman, if the right man comes a-wooing."

Only by feeling the vibrations of the piano does Helen Keller have a sense of the music.

· · · · ·

As usual, Bell knew Helen better than she knew herself. In 1916, the right man did come a-wooing. By then, Helen was the author of three more books, as well as magazine articles, essays and poems. She and Teacher had bought a handsome house in 1903 on seven acres of land in Wrentham, Massachusetts, purchased with profits from Helen's autobiography and the sale of some stock that Helen had been given. In 1913, the two women had launched a career on the lecture circuit. (Teacher and John Macy's marriage broke up in 1914.)

The right man, Peter Fagan, had first worked as John Macy's assistant and then as Helen's secretary. One summer evening in 1916, Peter, who had learned both Braille and the manual language, came into Helen's study and proposed marriage. Helen described the scene. "For a long time he held my hand in silence, then he began talking to me tenderly. I was surprised that he cared so much about me. There was sweet comfort in his loving words. I listened all a-tremble. He was full of plans for my happiness. He said if I would marry him, he would always be near to help me in the difficulties of life." Helen accepted Peter's proposal and they made plans to marry. "His love was a bright sun that shone upon my helplessness and isolation. The sweetness of being in love enchanted me."

But the Keller family was utterly opposed. Mrs. Keller was especially set against the match, perhaps because Helen was thirty-six and Peter was twenty-nine. More likely, however, Mrs. Keller objected because she felt that Peter, who was an outspoken radical, encouraged Helen's own radical tendencies. Whatever the reason, fate played into Mrs. Keller's hands. Teacher was sick and about to be hospitalized, which meant that Helen had no choice but to travel to Montgomery, Alabama, with her mother to stay temporarily at her sister Mildred's house. Although Mrs. Keller foiled an elopement attempt on the trip south, she wasn't able to prevent Peter from following Helen to Montgomery.

Helen and Peter met secretly one evening, but Mildred saw them together and summoned her husband, who ordered Peter to leave at gunpoint. Even looking down the barrel of a gun, Peter was courageous enough to announce that he and Helen were determined to marry. Only a few nights later Mildred and her husband again heard noises on their front porch. It was Helen. She and Peter had made plans to elope, an elopement that never came to pass for reasons that neither Helen nor anyone else ever revealed. All that is known is that Helen waited in her dark, silent world all night for a lover who never came, or if he did come, left without her.

"The brief love will remain in my life, a little island of joy surrounded by dark waters," Helen declared. "I am glad that I have had the experience of being loved and desired."

Only "my oldest friend," as Helen called Bell, had dreamed for Helen that she could find happiness in a loving marriage. But it was not to be. For the rest of her life, Helen's warmth and love were showered on family and friends . . . and one friend in particular. When Helen's autobiography, *The Story of My Life*, was published to great acclaim, the dedication read:

TO
ALEXANDER GRAHAM BELL

*W H O has taught the deaf to speak
and enabled the listening ear to hear
speech from the Atlantic to the Rockies,*

I DEDICATE
this Story of My Life.

. . . . .

CHAPTER 8

HELEN AND BELL saw less and less of each other as time went by, but they kept in touch with what the other was doing by way of letters, not to mention by way of articles and stories written about the two of them. And there was a lot written.

Although Bell's kite flying never did lead anywhere, he quickly foresaw the practical use of tetrahedral forms in construction. In 1902, he jotted down in his workbook that the tetrahedral form would be used "for all sorts of constructing—a new method of architecture. May prove a substitute for arches—& bridge work generally." Unfortunately, it was an idea whose time had not yet come. It wasn't until the 1940s that what became known as space frame architecture was successfully reinvented without any knowledge of Bell's original work.

But Bell never gave up striving, not even as he grew older. He believed that no one ages "who continues to observe, to remember what he observes, and to seek answers for his unceasing hows and whys about things." His Rule of Three was "Observe! Remember! Compare!" Only eight months before he died, Bell declared: "I cannot hope to work out half the problems in which I am interested."

In 1907, Bell launched five years of manned flight experiments, followed by work on hydrofoil boats that skimmed

Even toward the end of his life, Bell continues to work long hours.

* * * * *

above the water at high speeds. (In 1919 one of Bell's hydrofoil boats traveled over seventy miles an hour to set a world's marine record which stood for ten years.) Bell kept up his interest in the National Geographic Society and in breeding sheep for hereditary characteristics. While in his seventies, he returned to earlier projects, measuring ocean depths by bouncing echoes off the ocean floor and attempting to distill fresh water from seawater. Because Bell's first love had always been his work with the deaf, to the very end of his life he kept close ties with the Volta Bureau, the American Association for the Promotion of the Teaching of Speech to the Deaf and the Clarke School for the Deaf.

Helen Keller never gave up striving either. After graduating from Radcliffe, she had to get down to the serious business of supporting both Annie Sullivan and herself. "Write, speak, study, do whatever you possibly can. The more you accomplish, the more you will help the deaf everywhere," Bell advised her. "There are unique tasks waiting for you, a unique woman."

But Helen was becoming increasingly frustrated. "I found myself utterly confined to one subject—myself, and it was not long before I had exhausted it," she complained. Ever since her teens, Helen had been concerned with social reform, and that was what she wanted to write and talk about as an adult. "I have always been interested in all kinds of practical work to lessen human suffering," she pointed out.

Helen's first crusade was for legislation that would require that newborn infants' eyes be treated with silver nitrate drops to prevent blindness. "Those little ones cannot speak for themselves. Out of unimaginable darkness and silence I speak for them," was Helen's moving plea to a Congressman. As the years went by, Helen's political views became more and more liberal and in 1909, she joined the Socialist Party. Soon she was urging the government to provide jobs for the handicapped, arguing against capital punishment, protesting child labor and taking a strong stand against entering World War I, all radical ideas in the early 1900s.

Above all, Helen fought for woman's suffrage, or the right of women to vote. Calling herself a "militant suffragette," Helen asserted: "The women of America . . . cannot hope to get anything unless they are willing to fight and suffer for it." And Helen was willing to fight. In 1913, she was to have spoken at a suffrage demonstration in Washington, D.C., that was broken up by an angry mob while the police did nothing to stop the violence.

Although everyone loved the demure, smiling young Helen Keller, few were interested in what the outspoken, defiant adult Helen Keller had to say about America's problems. And that made Helen angry. "When I write seriously about the broader aspects of human life, people are apt to laugh, and tell me that I know nothing about the practical world," she objected.

Bell, who had invented the telephone when he was only twenty-nine, knew exactly how Helen felt at being confined to a single subject. "One would think I had never done anything worthwhile but the telephone," he once confided to her. Sympathetic to Helen's frustration, Bell urged her to speak out. "You must not put me among those who think that nothing you have to say about the affairs of the universe would be interesting," he commented. "I want to see you come out of yourself and write of the great things outside."

Many years after Bell's death, Helen recalled how much Bell's encouragement had meant to her. "I knew he considered me a capable human being, and not some sort of pitiable human ghost groping its way through the world. Is it any wonder that I loved him?"

The two friends' political viewpoint ran along similar lines, although Bell was never as radical or militant as Helen. Nevertheless, like Helen, Bell strongly upheld the right of women to vote. (He and Mabel had been supporters of the 1913 woman's suffrage parade in Washington when a mob had prevented Helen from speaking.) Both Helen and Bell believed that the federal government should take an active role in helping the handicapped, minority groups and those in need. Bell observed "that as the Government is of the people by the people and for the people, it is bound to provide for its starving members."

Although Helen became increasingly involved with the cause of the blind rather than the deaf, she and Bell were always available to one another. "I need you," Helen telegraphed Bell at his Washington home in January of 1907 when she was about to give a speech in New York City. "Teacher has bad cold and cannot speak. Will you stand beside me and repeat my speech so that all may hear." Despite a previous commitment in Ohio, Bell dropped everything and hurried to New York. A reporter noted: "Miss Keller rose to a great burst of applause and was led to the centre of the stage by Professor Alexander Graham Bell." Bell's unexpected appearance, plus his incomparable voice, was doubtless a happy addition to the program.

With Helen's writing earning less and less, in 1912 she and Teacher made the decision to give lectures around the country for pay. In preparation, Helen again took voice lessons. As soon as Bell heard about the voice lessons, he called on Helen for a favor. Could she please speak at the ninth annual meeting of the Association in Providence, Rhode Island? Of course she would.

"My friends seemed delighted with the results," Helen wrote to her mother afterwards. "Dr. Bell was there and his enthusiasm made me very happy." Bell was indeed enthusiastic. "I am perfectly astonished in the change in Helen's voice," he told the Association members, adding that the improvement in Helen's speech was "great, good news" for all teachers of the deaf.

But speaking to a friendly Association membership was quite different from lecturing to a paying audience, and when Helen first stepped onto the lecture stage in February of 1913, she froze. "I stood cold, riveted, trembling, voiceless," she revealed. "At last I forced a sound. It felt to me like a cannon going off, but they told me afterwards it was a mere whisper." When she was finished, she wept, sure that she had let everyone down. Little could she know that her career in public speaking would last another fifty years.

In July of 1918, it was Helen's turn to ask Bell for a favor . . . a big favor. Hollywood was making a movie of her life called *Deliverance* and Helen wanted Bell to appear in it. "Dear Dr. Bell, it would be such a happiness to have you beside me in

A poster advertising the movie *Deliverance* features
its star, Helen Keller.

· · · · ·

my picture-travels," she wrote, not above drawing on old memories to entice him. "Even before my teacher came to me, you held out a warm hand to me in the dark. Indeed, it was through you that she came to me. How vividly it all comes back!" She signed the letter "Affectionately your friend, Helen Keller."

But Bell was now seventy-one, the summer heat bothered him more than ever and the thought of acting in a movie appealed to him not at all. Nevertheless, if Helen really needed him, he would do it. "It is a letter which would move a heart of stone and it has touched me deeply," he replied. "It brings back recollections of the little girl I met in Washington so long ago, and you are still that little girl to me. I can only say that anything you want me to do I will do for your sake . . . Your loving friend, Alexander Graham Bell." (Fortunately, he was never needed.)

With the movie a box office failure and the onset of World War I putting an end to their lecture tours, Helen and Teacher again found themselves short of money. Although they had turned down earlier offers to go into vaudeville, they now agreed to give it a try. In 1920, Helen and Teacher began to travel around the country appearing on the vaudeville stage. "At first it seemed strange to find ourselves on a program with dancers, acrobats and trained animals," Helen confessed. However, she also had to confess that she rather enjoyed the excitement and carnival atmosphere. Furthermore, their vaudeville act was only twenty minutes long instead of the hour and a half required for a lecture and they stayed in one place for a week instead of just a day. Plus, their audiences were wildly enthusiastic.

Helen and Teacher's act was much like their lectures. Teacher would first talk about her arrival in Tuscumbia and how the young Helen Keller learned the meaning of language. Helen would then place her hand on Teacher's lips to show how she read Teacher's speech, after which she would speak briefly. Questions from the audience followed. Although Helen was criticized for appearing in vaudeville, she never felt any shame in doing honest work for honest wages. Besides, she and

Helen Keller, Anne Sullivan Macy, and Polly Thomson, their secretary, (left to right) dress formally for their vaudeville act.

· · · · ·

Teacher made more money than they had lecturing. "I am paying my own passage through the world and I am proud of it," Helen boasted.

Helen and Bell met for the last time in 1920. Bell had just returned from a long trip to Scotland and England with his wife and granddaughter for what he called a "farewell visit." It turned out to be an unhappy journey back into time. Almost everyone Bell had known was dead, familiar neighborhoods were gone and Bell returned depressed and feeling old. "I was a stranger in my own land," he mourned.

Helen, too, sensed that Bell's life was drawing to a close. "The last time I saw him he was on his way home from a visit to Edinburgh," she recalled. "I felt very sad when I said good-by to him. I had a presentiment that I should not see him again in this life." And she didn't.

On August 2, 1922, at the age of seventy-five, Bell died quietly in his sleep at Beinn Bhreagh, his wife Mabel at his side. Two days later, on August 4, Bell was buried high on a hill overlooking Bras d'Or Lake. Some years later, Helen revealed that on one of her visits to Beinn Bhreagh, Bell had taken her to that very site. "Once he had pointed out that spot to me, and quoted Browning's verse: 'Here is the place, Helen, where I shall sleep the last sleep' / 'Where meteors shoot, clouds form, Lightnings are loosened, Stars come and go!'"

As a tribute to Bell, at the exact time of his burial, all telephone service in the United States was halted for one minute. For most Americans, it was a taste of the kind of isolation that people everywhere had experienced before Bell uttered his famous command: "Mr. Watson—Come here—I want to see you."

But Bell had broken down more barriers than could be overcome by the telephone. As his first priority, Bell had devoted his life to bringing the deaf into the speaking and hearing world. "I am proud to think that I have been a teacher of the deaf," he stated. But his work had been frustrating, too. "I wish my experiences had resulted in enabling the deaf to speak with less difficulty. That would have made me truly happy," Bell once told Helen. But Helen, more than anyone else, knew how much Bell had accomplished. "The noble friendship of Dr. Bell towards the deaf has enriched countless silent lives," she wrote after his death. "Every teacher of the deaf . . . has been influenced by Dr. Bell."

Helen Keller, too, spent her life breaking down barriers, barriers that prevented the handicapped from being accepted as full members of society. And Bell's unfailing support had spurred her on. "You can do anything you think you can. Remember that many will be brave in your courage," he had counseled. It was true. Perhaps more than any other achievement, Helen changed attitudes. The example of her very public life of courage, determination and good humor not only changed attitudes of people toward the handicapped, but it also changed attitudes of the handicapped towards themselves.

Among the most famous individuals of their time, Alexander Graham Bell and Helen Keller were mythic figures in the eyes of the public. But they were never that to each other. Until his death, Bell had rallied to Helen's side whenever he sensed that she needed him. "You have always shown a father's joy in my successes and a father's tenderness when things have not gone right," she wrote Bell in 1918.

Helen may not have realized it, but she had been just as important to Bell. At every turn, Helen had been willing to stand as proof that what Bell had always fought for could be accomplished. The handicapped, especially the deaf, could lead independent lives, form meaningful relationships and above all make a useful contribution to the world in which they lived.

Over and beyond what each did to help the other, Helen and Bell were friends in the deepest sense. They cared for one another, shared good times as well as bad, and were attuned to each other's dreams and concerns. Death may have separated them, but to the end of her life, Helen never forgot the "warm hand" that Bell had held out to her in the dark. In 1929, she wrote an article about Bell with a title that said it all: "If You Have Friends You Can Endure Anything: The Story of My Great Debt to Dr. Alexander Graham Bell." In it, she wrote: "I remember him not so much as a great inventor, or as a great benefactor, but simply as a wise, affectionate, and understanding friend."

Many years after Bell's death, Helen chanced to meet one of Bell's granddaughters during a trip to Japan and their talk naturally turned to memories of Bell. Reflecting on what Bell and his friendship had meant to her, Helen said simply, "I still hunger for the touch of his dear hand in mine."

EPILOGUE

. . . . .

TWO YEARS after Bell's death, in 1924, Helen Keller began what she called her "life-work." Traveling around the country, and the world, she became a fund-raiser for the American Foundation for the Blind and for the Overseas Foundation for the Blind.

As the years passed, Annie Sullivan became increasingly blind and ill. After serving as Helen's teacher and beloved companion for almost fifty years, Annie Sullivan died on October 20, 1936. Polly Thomson, a young Scotswoman who had first come to work for Helen and Teacher as a secretary in 1914, picked up where Teacher had left off, acting as Helen's companion until her own death in 1960.

Although she was already in her sixties, during World War II Helen Keller took on a new role. From 1943 through 1946, she visited military hospitals, both in the United States and overseas, giving hope and courage to wounded and handicapped service men and women. It was, she said, "the crowning experience of my life."

On her eightieth birthday, Helen Keller was asked what her plans for the future were. She replied, "I will always—as long as I have breath—work for the handicapped." Eight years later, on June 1, 1968, Helen Keller died.

BIBLIOGRAPHY

. . . . .

Baida, Peter. "Breaking the Connection." *American Heritage.* June/July 1985. Vol. 36, No. 4, p. 65.

Barnett, Lincoln. "The Voice Heard Round the World." *American Heritage.* Vol. XVI, No. 3, April 1965, p. 50.

Bell, Alexander Graham. "Prehistoric Telephone Days." *The National Geographic.* Vol. XLI, No. 3, March 1922, p. 223.

Braddy, Nella. *Anne Sullivan Macy: The Story Behind Helen Keller.* Garden City, New York: Doubleday, Doran & Company, 1933.

Bruce, Robert V. "A Conquest of Solitude." *American Heritage.* Vol. XXIV, No. 3, April 1973, p. 28.

——— "Alexander Graham Bell." *The National Geographic.* Vol. 174, No. 3, September 1988, p. 358.

——— *Bell: Alexander Graham Bell and the Conquest of Solitude.* Boston: Little, Brown, 1973.

Eber, Dorothy Harley. *Genius at Work.* New York: The Viking Press, 1982.

Fifty-Seventh Annual Report of the Trustees of the Perkins Institution and Massachusetts School for the Blind. September 30, 1888. Boston: Wright & Potter Printing Co., State Printers, 1889.

Fifty-Sixth Annual Report of the Trustees of the Perkins Institution and Massachusetts School for the Blind. September 30, 1887. Boston: Wright & Potter Printing Co., State Printers, 1888.

Grosvenor, Lilian. "Clarke School." *The National Geographic.* Vol. CVII, #3, March 1955, p. 379.

Keller, Helen. "An Apology for Going to College." *McClure's Magazine.* June 1905, p. 190.

———— "A Chat About the Hand." *Century Magazine.* Vol. 69, No. 3, 1905, p. 455.

———— "Helen Keller Addresses Pioneers." Western Electric, December 1928, p. 12.

———— *Helen Keller's Journal.* Garden City, New York: Doubleday, Doran & Company, Inc., 1938.

———— "If You Have Friends You Can Endure Anything: The Story of my Great Debt to Alexander Graham Bell." *The American Magazine.* September 1929, p. 62.

———— *Midstream: My Later Life.* New York: The Crowell Publishing Company, 1929.

———— "My Animal Friends." *Zoological Society Bulletin.* Vol. XXV, No. 5, September 1923, p. 111.

———— *Optimism.* New York: T. Y. Crowell and Company, 1903.

———— *Out of the Dark.* Garden City, New York: Doubleday, Page & Company, 1913.

———— "Sense and Sensibility." *Century Magazine.* Vol. 75, No. 4, 1908, p. 566.

———— *The Story of My Life.* Garden City, New York: Doubleday, Page & Company, 1903.

———— *Teacher: Anne Sullivan Macy.* Garden City, New York: Doubleday & Company, 1955.

———— *The World I Live In.* New York: The Century Company, 1904.

Lash, Joseph P. *Helen and Teacher: The Story of Helen Keller and Anne Sullivan Macy.* New York: Dell Publishing Co., 1980.

Lesage, Jean. "Alexander Graham Bell Museum: Tribute to a Genius." *The National Geographic.* Vol. CX, No. 2, August 1956, p. 227.

Sixtieth Annual Report of the Trustees of the Perkins Institution and Massachusetts School for the Blind. September 30, 1891. Boston: Wright & Potter Printing Co., State Printers, 1892.

Watson, Thomas A. *Exploring Life: The Autobiography of Thomas A. Watson.* New York: D. Appleton and Company, 1926.

Helen Keller Folders. Helen Keller Archives, American Foundation for the Blind, New York.

Alexander Graham Bell Correspondence. The Library of Congress, Washington, D.C.

Alexander Graham Bell and Helen Keller Correspondence. The Volta Bureau Library, Alexander Graham Bell Association for the Deaf, Washington, D.C.

INDEX

. . . . .

Alexander Graham Bell"
(Helen Keller), 87–88

K

Keller, Arthur H. (father), 7, 25,
27, 28, 38, 44, 53, 55, 56, 69
Bell, takes Helen to meet, 8, 23,
25
death of, 59
publicity, dislike of, 30
Keller, Eveline (aunt), 7, 8, 30
Keller, Helen
American Association for the
Promotion of the Teaching of
Speech to the Deaf and, 49–50,
56, 82
American Foundation for the
Blind and, 89
autobiography (*The Story of My
Life*), 27, 38, 74, 75, 77
at Cambridge School for Young
Ladies, 57, 59
death of, 89
education of, 25, 27–28, 30,
32–34, 36, 38–39, 41–44,
46–47, 49–50, 52–57, 59,
61–62, 66, 68–70, 73–74, 80
fame, 30, 32, 39, 47, 49–50,
62
Frost King, 39, 41, 44, 59, 70
as Fuller's student, 38
girlhood years, 7–8, 23–25,
27–28, 30, 32–34, 36, 38–39,
41–44, 46–47, 49–50, 52–56,
69, 70
Helen Keller Souvenir, 39, 59
"If You Have Friends You Can
Endure Anything: The Story of
My Great Debt to Dr.
Alexander Graham Bell,"
87–88
Lecture circuit 82, 84–86
marriage, possibility of, 73–77

movie of her life (*Deliverance*),
82, 84
Niagara Falls, 46, 48
Overseas Foundation for the
Blind and, 89
at Perkins Institute for the Blind,
34, 36, 39, 41, 70
Radcliffe College and, 56–57, 59,
61–62, 69, 70, 73, 74, 80
Socialist Party and, 80
speech of, 8, 24, 25, 38–39, 54,
56, 82
Swedenborgianism and, 41
trust fund for, 56, 66
woman's suffrage and, 80–81
at Wright-Humanson School for
the Deaf, 53–54, 56
Vaudeville, 84, 85
See also Keller-Bell relationship;
Keller-Sullivan relationship
Keller, Mildred (sister), 25, 76
Keller, Mrs. (mother), 8, 24, 25, 28,
34, 46, 55, 56, 59, 69, 73, 82
Helen's marriage opposed by,
76
publicity, dislike of, 30
Keller-Bell relationship
Aleck's comments on Helen, 41,
57, 74, 82
correspondence, 30, 62, 69, 78,
82, 84, 87
financial support for, 55–56, 66
first meeting, 8, 23, 25
Helen's comments on Aleck, 8,
23, 33, 36, 42–44, 46, 49, 56,
62, 66, 68–70, 81, 82, 87–88
visits, 8, 23, 25, 33–34, 42–44,
46, 47, 49–50, 52–53, 55–57,
66, 68–70, 73–75, 78, 82, 86
Keller-Sullivan relationship
Helen's comments on Annie, 30,
34, 43, 49–50
separation, possibility of, 57, 59

as teacher/student and friends, 27–28, 30, 32–34, 38, 39, 41–44, 46–47, 49–50, 52–57, 59, 61–62, 71, 73–76, 80, 82, 84, 86, 89

M

Macy, John, 74–76
Manual alphabet, 11, 23, 27, 28, 29, 30, 31, 63, 76
Montessori, Maria, 44
Morse code, 38

N

National Geographic Society, 65, 66, 80

O

Overseas Foundation for the Blind, 89

P

Perkins Institute for the Blind, 23, 25, 27, 30, 70
Helen at, 34, 36, 39, 41

R

Radcliffe College, 56–57, 59, 61–62, 69, 70, 73, 74, 80
Rochester School for the Deaf, 44

S

Sanders, Thomas, 17, 18
Sign language, 13, 27
Socialist Party, 80

Story of My Life, The (Helen Keller's autobiography), 27, 38, 74, 75, 77
Stringer, Tommy, 34, 36
Sullivan, Anne Mansfield (Annie) ("Teacher")
Bell, comments on, 43, 49–50, 55–56
brother of, 27, 43
death of, 89
girlhood years, 25, 27, 43
Macy, marriage to, 74–75
mother of, 25, 43
See also Keller-Sullivan relationship
Swedenborgianism, 41

T

Thomson, Polly, 89
Twain, Mark, 41, 44

V

Victoria, queen of England, 20
Visible Speech alphabet, 10, 13, 15, 17, 21
Volta Bureau, 34, 39, 41, 44, 59, 80
Volta Laboratory, 20
Volta Prize, 20

W

Watson, Thomas, 10, 17, 18, 65, 86
Woman's suffrage, 81
Wright-Humanson School for the Deaf, 53–54, 56

PHOTOGRAPH CREDITS

. . . . .

Alexander Graham Bell Association for the deaf, p. 46
American Foundation for the Blind, pp. 9, 29, 31, 48, 58, 60, 85.
Library of Congress, pp. 12, 14, 16, 19, 21, 22, 45, 51, 53, 63, 64, 67, 68, 71, 72, 75, 79.
Perkins School for the Blind, pp. 26, 35, 37, 40, 83.